Let there be Lights

Chelsea Kong

Let there be Lights
Published in the United States of America
Copyright 2024
Chelsea Kong

All rights reserved. No part of this work is transferrable, either in whole or in part. It may not be reproduced, stored in a retrieval system, or transmitted in any form or by any means, electronic, mechanical photocopying, recording, or otherwise, without the express prior written permission of both the copyright owner and this publisher. Scanning, uploading, and distribution of this book via any means whatsoever is illegal and punishable by law.

This book is created using stock images from Adobe, Deposit Photos, and created in Photoshop.

Happy Hanukkah

MAY LOVE AND LIGHT FILL YOUR HEART

What is the Festival of Lights?

The Festival of Lights begins on Kislev 25 and is eight days long.

In the Western calendar, it falls in November or December.

The word Hanukkah means "dedication" and is related to lights.

It's celebrated around the same time as Christmas to mark the rededication of the Temple in 165 B.C.

Chanukkuh

The feast is also called Hanukkah, which Jewish children celebrate instead of Christmas to remind them about the Dedication of the Temple after the revolt led by Judas Maccabeus against the Greek-Syrian Selucid empire.

What God's Word Says

The time came for the Feast of Dedication at Jerusalem.

This was during the winter. Jesus was walking in the Temple in Solomon's Porch. (John 10:22-23)

God will shake the nations and fill the temple with His glory (Haggai 2:7).

God said that He will make the later Temple greater than the past one (Haggai 2:9).

Why Celebrate?

The celebration reminds God's people of the Temple of God.

It reminds them of the dark times when they were being chased by their enemies.

God wanted His people to remember Him.

It points to Jesus who makes us clean by His blood.

He is the Light of the World.

When Does It Start?

Hanukkah begins on the eve of Kislev 25 in the Jewish calendar, often falls about the same time as December 23.

Kislev is the ninth month of the Jewish Calendar and is usually 30 days long. It can start in late November and continue to late December. We need to check the Jewish calendar to know the exact dates as it changes.

Kislev means 'hope or trust 'and is called the "month of dreams."

Celebration for Eight Days

Women are to stop the housework every evening. They are to light the lights each night.

Women light the Hanukkah menorah (lampstand) because they are part of the miracle.

It became a holiday in the dark times.

Children get gifts.

Menorah

The menorah is the candlestand used for lighting the candles.

It has nine candles on it. One candle is used to light the other candles from left to right. This candle also sits taller than the others.

It reminds us of Jesus Christ, who gives us light.

A blessing is said when lighting the candle each night.

Blessing 2: Miracles

The second blessing spoken is:

Baruch atah Adonai, Eloheinu melech haolam, she-asah nisim laavoteinu v'imoteinu bayamim hahaeim baz'man hazeh.

(Blessed are You, Adonai our God, Ruler of the Universe, who performed wondrous deeds for our ancestors in those ancient days at this season.)

Blessing 3:
First Night of Hanukkah Prayer

The third blessing spoken is:

Baruch atah Adonai, Eloheinu melech haolam, shehecheyanu v'kiy'manu v'higiyanu laz'man hazeh.

(Blessed are You, Adonai our God, Ruler of the Universe, who has kept us alive, sustained us, and brought us to this season.)

The menorah is put in the front window for everyone to see.

Sing Songs

Songs are sung on Hanukkah.

It's good to sing a new song to the Lord.

It is a great time to sing praises to Him.

Dreidel Game

Children play a game of dreidel, which is a spinning top.

The game originates in ancient Greece and Rome.

Children come together and get gelt and chocolate coins for poker chips.

They take turns spinning the dreidel to win or get nothing.

Dreidel Words

Each time they spin, the dreidel will create words.

It tells about the Hanukkah story.

A great miracle happened there.

Children can win half a pot or lose some gelt.

Food

There are traditional foods made with oil. It is the time of the miracle of the oil.

There are foods made with cheese.

Cheese Latkes and Sauces

Among the foods are cheese latkes, as well as potato latkes cooked in oil.

These are served with sour cream and applesauce.

Braided Egg Bread

There is one bread called challah that Jews eat to celebrate.

It is sweet and made with sugar.
It is eaten with cheese.

Doughnuts

Jews also eat sufganiyot, or doughnuts fried in oil.
There are also the smaller doughnuts that look like balls.

Other Items

On the table there is also a bottle of wine and a bottle of oil.

This is usually served with parched corn,

dry figs, bread, and cheese.

This was during the winter. Jesus was walking in the Temple in Solomon's Porch. (John 10:22-23)

God will shake the nations and fill the temple with His glory (Haggai 2:7).

God said that He will make the later Temple greater than the past one (Haggai 2:9).

The people wanted to know if He was the Messiah.
He told them that they must believe in the Father.
Believe in God's Words.

Jesus the Messiah

Jesus is the Messiah that God promised.
He died on the cross for all the sins of the world.

It is by His blood that we are clean from sin.

He gave us a new life to dedicate to God.

Have a blessed Hanukkah!

Activités

Word Search

Blessing
Doughnuts
Dreidel
Games
Gifts

Hanukkah
Lights
Menorah
Miracles
Temple

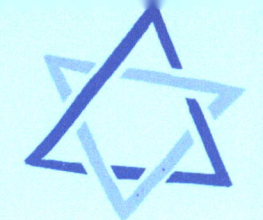

Word Search

V	L	Z	D	U	N	L	A	K	S
C	B	L	E	S	S	I	N	G	T
S	T	C	O	A	Q	G	I	J	U
H	E	J	X	T	R	F	V	C	N
A	M	L	Q	D	T	T	E	P	H
N	P	D	C	S	J	S	M	K	G
U	L	Y	H	A	B	Z	A	B	U
K	E	F	T	J	R	U	G	Y	O
K	M	B	L	E	D	I	E	R	D
A	H	A	R	O	N	E	M	Z	J
H	D	W	J	Q	J	C	U	K	S

Crossword

Crossword

Across

1. This is said during the 8 days celebration.

3. Children get to play these and dreidels.

6. Families celebrate this festival every year in November or in December.

Down

2. It is lit for Hanukkah.

4. Hanukkah is also called the Festival of _____

5. A dessert that is sweet and round.

Answers

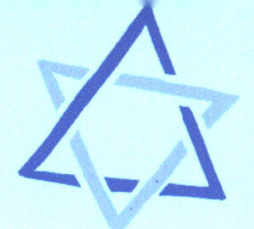

Word Search

V	L	Z	D	U	N	L	A	K	S
C	B	L	E	S	S	I	N	G	T
S	T	C	O	A	Q	G	I	J	U
H	E	J	X	T	R	F	V	C	N
A	M	L	Q	D	T	T	E	P	H
N	P	D	C	S	J	S	M	K	G
U	L	Y	H	A	B	Z	A	B	U
K	E	F	T	J	R	U	G	Y	O
K	M	B	L	E	D	I	E	R	D
A	H	A	R	O	N	E	M	Z	J
H	D	W	J	Q	J	C	U	K	S

Crossword

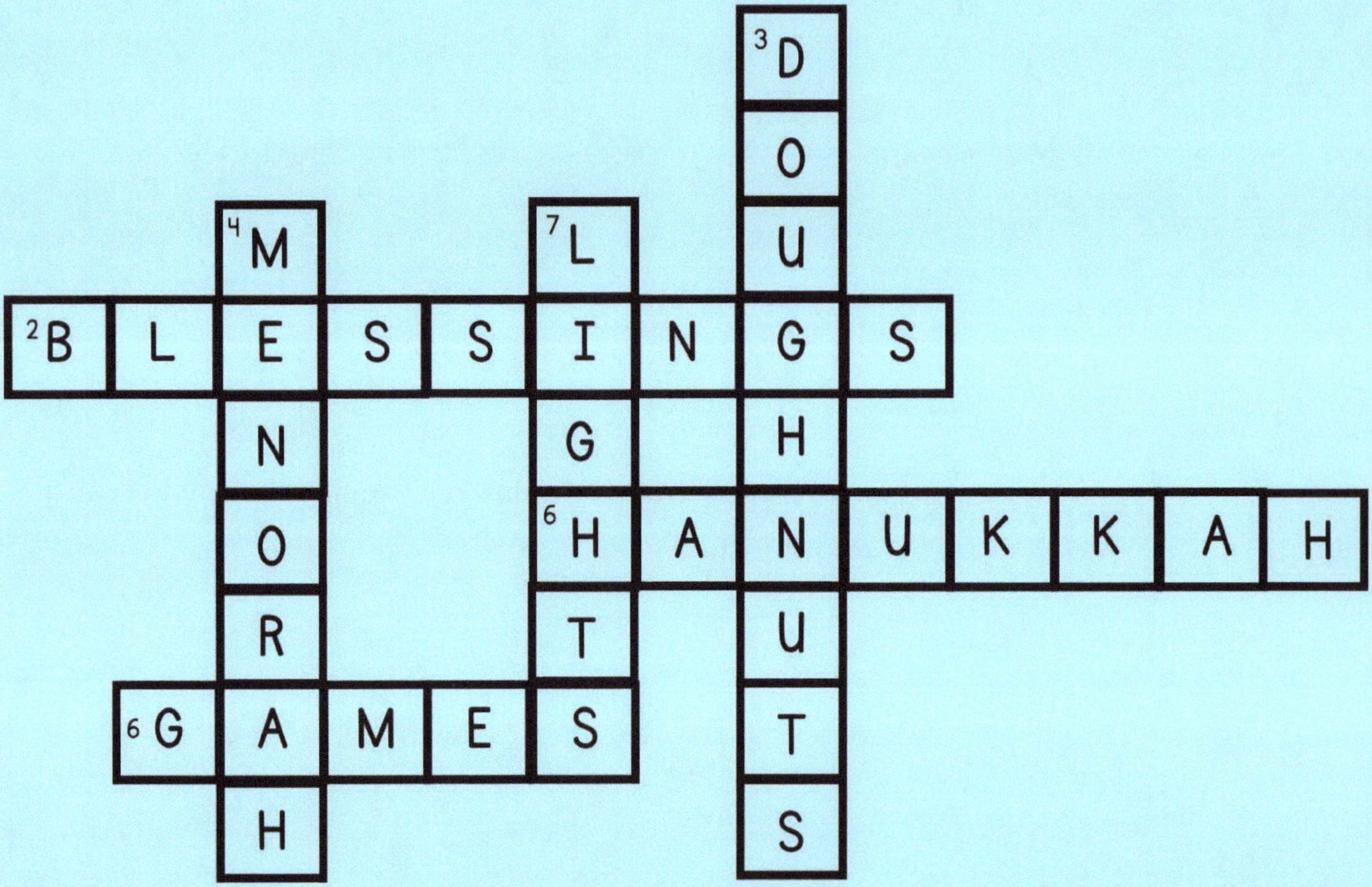

2 BLESSINGS
3 DOUGHNUTS
4 MENORAH
6 HANUKKAH
6 GAMES
7 LIGHTS

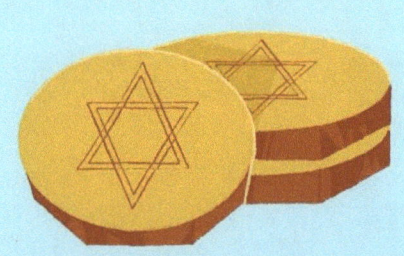

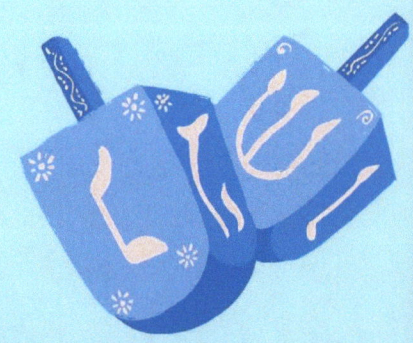

SALVATION PRAYER

God, I know I sinned against you. Forgive me for the wrong that I have done. I believe that Jesus Christ died on the cross for me. That He rose from the grave so that after three days. I can have His long-lasting life. Come into my heart to be my Lord and Savior. I choose to turn away from my sins and I choose to follow you. Lead me to walk with you. Keep me safe and teach me your ways. Stop every bad thing in my life that has an open door to hurt me. Close those doors. Holy Spirit, fill me now in Jesus' name. Amen.

BAPTISM IN THE HOLY SPIRIT

Jesus, you are the one that fills me with Your Spirit. Come Holy Spirit and come into my life and fill me to overflow with Your presence. Come with your fire too. Thank you for the gift of tongues in Jesus' name. Amen.

Open your mouth and let the words come out that God gives you. It will be words that you don't know what they mean. You can ask God what it means. You need to let Him talk through you every day to grow this gift.

He will bring you closer to God and you will know Jesus more. You will have power from God to do great things and know things.

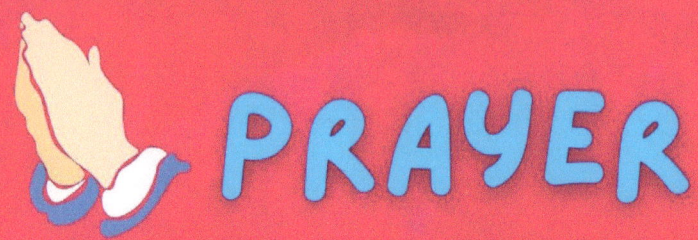
PRAYER

Father God, remind me of what Jesus has done. I dedicate my life to Jesus. Thank you for saving me. Thank you for Your light that breaks the darkness. Thank you that You are the Savior of the world. Thank you for protection in Jesus' name. Amen.

Message from the Author

Thank you for reading this book. I hope you can leave a good review to encourage me to write more books to teach children and adults. This was a fun book to write. The Festival of Lights or Hanukkah is celebrated by both Jews and Christians in the world. Christians celebrate it symbolically. They believe that Jesus Christ is the Light of the world. Messianic Jews also believe this and celebrate Hanukkah in remembrance of Yeshua (Jesus Christ). They also call him Messiah. Not all Jews accept this, so this book is to share how they celebrate this feast or festival. It is written for Messianic Jews and Christians.

OTHER PRODUCTS

Knowing God
How to Hear God's Voice
New Life in Jesus
Loving Israel
God's Gifts/Spiritual Talents
Meeting God
Word Power
Fruit of the Spirit
The Tabernacle
Bride for Jesus
A Life of Prayer
Live Free
Who am I in Jesus
Walk in Love
God's Favor
Man of God
Woman of God
How to Use Money

God's Wisdom
Fasting
See Jerusalem and Bethany
First Fruit Offering
Feast of Trumpets
Day of Atonement
Feast of Tabernacles
Counting the Omer
Festival of Lights
Glory, Presence, and Holy Spirit
Live in God's Presence
Pentecost
See Galilee, Nazareth, and Tiberias
Hear God Speak
Knowing Jesus
Knowing Holy Spirit
A Healthy Life
Healthy Life Work Book

OTHER PRODUCTS

- Smokey the Cat
- Passover Unleavened Bread
- Resurrection Life
- The Blessing
- Revival
- Chelsea Learns Hebrew
- Thanksgiving
- Give Thanks
- Jesus Birth
- Loving Jesus: Bride and Groom
- Proverbs 31 Woman
- ABC of People in the Bible
- Colours in the Bible
- Breakthroughs
- Open Doors
- The Seven Spirits of God
- Numbers in the Bible
- Aglee the Eagle
- An Eagle's Life
- Chelsea Learns Numbers in Hebrew
- ABC's of Faith
- Feast of Purim
- A Royal Life

OTHER PRODUCTS

Devotionals
31 Day Devotional

Inspirational/Other
Chelsea's Psalms and Poems
Your Daily Meal: Chelsea's Photo Album
Chelsea's Psalms and Poems2

Puzzle Books
Biblical Puzzle Book Vol 1-5
Bible Puzzles for Young Children Book 1-3
Biblical Puzzle for Children Books 1-5

OTHER PRODUCTS

Teaching Series

How to Hear God's Voice Teaching Guide & Audio Book

Relationship with God, Jesus, Holy Spirit Guide

Knowing God, Jesus, Holy Spirit Guide & Audio Book

Flowing in the Prophetic

Teaching (Non-Sale on my website)

Purim

Passover

Resurrection

BOOK REVIEWS

More books on Amazon, Kobo, and Barnes and Noble, Smashwords, and IngramSpark.
https://chelseak532002550.wordpress.com/

More books on Amazon, Kobo, and Barnes and Noble, Smashwords, and IngramSpark.
https://www.amazon.com/author/chelseakong

Please leave a review and share with friends to help the author continue to write more books to reach more readers. Thank you so much for your support.

Review!

About
CHELSEA KONG

She is a writer, creative arts and digital media artist, skilled administration and certified PCP (Payroll Compliance Professional), and podcaster. Chelsea also served in a variety of roles, from audiovisual, photography, to assisting on the worship team, and ministry team. She also has a passion for families being united.

Chelsea has been a guest on Unity Live Radio, The Lady Tracey Show, and How to Live for Christ and is highly recommended by a Proud Christian blog. She is also a guest blogger. A few of her books have been featured in YourAuthorHub, etc. She graduated from Hotel and Restaurant Management, Digital Media Arts, Office Administration, Payroll Compliance Professional, and experience working with children. Chelsea lives in Toronto, Canada. She mainly writes children's books, stories, bridal writing, poems, lyrics for songs, words of encouragement, blessings, prayers, and jokes. The author of How to Hear the Voice of God, the Bridal Collection, Knowing God, etc. She also has her own Bible Puzzle books and other inspired products. Her podcast channel is called Chelsea K on Anchor, Spotify, and iTunes.

Please check my website to find out more:
https://chelseak532002550.wordpress.com/

www.ingramcontent.com/pod-product-compliance
Lightning Source LLC
Chambersburg PA
CBHW041945110426
R18126000001B/R181260PG42743CBX00002B/3

9781998335640